I0530038

Split
Daughter
of Eve

Split Daughter of Eve © 2025 Catherine Gonick

Cover art: Sarah Savidge, *Incoming Mermaid*
Author photo: Morgan Donohue

ISBN PRINT: 978-1-962405-16-4
Library of Congress Control Number: 2025937251

Sheila-Na-Gig Editions
Russell, KY
Hayley Mitchell Haugen, Editor
www.sheilanagigblog.com

ALL RIGHTS RESERVED
Printed in the United States of America

Split
Daughter
of Eve

POEMS

Catherine Gonick

Sheila-Na-Gig Editions

Advance Praise for Split Daughter of Eve

Early in her remarkable first collection, Catherine Gonick announces that "cultural math/confounds." The speaker in these poems is confounded by the binaries that shape her life within what is an inherited culture. The list of binaries is long—mother/father, female/male/, Catholic/Jew, religious/atheist, protector/predator—and to the speaker none of these are simple or easy to understand. The title, *Split Daughter of Eve*, suggests at least one source of the problem. Unlike Eve, the mother who chooses to eat from the tree of knowledge, the daughter-speaker inherits whatever the progenitors have offered, a fait accompli. Eve cannot or will not protect this daughter who must figure it all out on her own. For Gonick, to be a woman is to be afraid existence is an ongoing state of split desire—both a longing for a protective mother (the image used is of an ancient and enveloping tree) as well as a longing for the erotic invitation of the father, something both tempting and frightening, a naked man cheerfully roaming a house filled with women. The speaker goes to "sacred spaces" and finds "an empty room." Solace comes from the fierce refusal to turn away from what's painful and confusing and difficult. In one poem the speaker describes climbing out of an abductor's car to avoid what might have been rape or murder or both. The speaker's courage and resourcefulness save her. By analogy Gonick knows that only by writing poems rather than explanations can she escape the binary traps. In doing so she does what poetry should do—instruct and delight. This book will stay with you; I recommend it highly.

—Ruth Danon, author of *Turn up the Heat*

Catherine Gonick scrutinizes, with ferocious reverence, what it means to embody multiple dualities: Christian and Jew, wife and lover, sister and daughter. She burrows into the fraught richness of legacy, re-visioning foundational stories and laying bare her attempts to "herd random angels"—of inheritance, of history— "with swift and furious gestures." These poems never fall back on platitude, but rather, revel in the contradictory tapestry of everything we are blessed to inherit.

—Kristen Holt-Browning, author of *The Only Animal Awake in the House* and *Ordinary Devotion*

Catherine Gonick is a poet of strength, skill, authenticity and soul. In this collection, she shoulders the task of trying to reconcile the cultural and religious misalignment in her upbringing that's complicated by the sexual malfunctioning in her childhood home. Somehow, the grace afforded by a heroic Holocaust survivor, and her life-long fascination with the charismatic Christ, pull her up from a well of darkness to end with a feeling of mild, unforced, unsentimental hope.

—Janet Ruhe-Schoen, author of *Rejoice in my Gladness: The Life of Táhirih.*

Acknowledgments

I am grateful to the editors who published poems included in this book. Some of the poems appeared in slightly different forms or with different titles.

Amethyst Review: "In the Orchards of Eden"
Beltway Poetry Quarterly: "Visiting the Convent at San Marco"
Dead of Winter 2021 (Milk & Cake Press): "When the Minotaur Was a Girl"
decomp: "Flash Frozen "
Evening Street Review: "At Cousin Fanny's Table"
Ginosko Literary Journal: "Entertaining the Troops"
Grabbed: Poets & Writers on Sexual Assault, Empowerment and Healing (Beacon Press): "Kidnapped Girls"
Halfway Down the Stairs: "First Purchase"
in plein air (Poetic License Press): "If a Tree Were Your Mother"
Live Encounters: "Brief for the Daughter"
Mediterranean Poetry: "Touring Topkapi Harem You Imagine"
Notre Dame Review: "Near the Exit"
Of the Book: "Newcomers," "Origin Story"
One Art: "Into the Woods," "Merging," "How I Became a Zionist Without Really Trying"
Pedestal: "Sister Mary Joseph Serves Lunch in Ávila"
PoetsArtists: "Cow of Plenty"
Second Coming: "Learning to See Through Atheist Eyes"
Silver Birch Press: "Memento Mori"
Soul-Lit: "Deus Absconditus," "Double in the House of the Lord"
The New Verse News: "Another False Narrative" (also published in *Support Ukraine*, Moonstone Press), "Warfare is the Opposite of Practicing Tonglen"
The Nu Review: "Invention of the One God," "Getting Wings"
The Orchards Poetry Journal: "Eating Figs in a Field Between Ranch Houses"
Word Riot: "Minnesota Christmas"

I am also grateful to the many friends and fellow writers who provided years of literary and other kinds of support needed to bring this book into the world, including Ruth Danon, Rhonda Donohue, Lawrence Dorfman, Amy Shorr, Jill Cook, Indran Amirthanayagam, Natania Rosenfeld, Janet Ruhe-Schoen, Kristen Holt-Browning, Dr. Claudia Fidanque, Lisa Seidenberg, William Moorhead, Ralph Nazareth, Barry Fruchter, and Glen Vecchione. I thank Sarah Savidge for creating the art used for the cover. I am deeply grateful to Hayley Mitchell Haugen of Sheila-Na-Gig Editions for accepting my work and for her dedication and professionalism. Finally, I thank my sister, Jean Gonick, and my husband, Marshall Mermell, who have stood by me all the way.

For all my family members, past and present

Contents

I. Birthrights

II. Dangers

III. Margins of Safety

I. Birthrights

The Color of Holiness

White slime surrounded the yolk
of the soft-boiled egg.

Couldn't I please just cover it up
with some jelly?

Statue-face in a stiff white coif,
the cafeteria nun said No.

Prayer denied, I dug my spoon
into the yellow, let a morsel of hate

slide down my throat.
A moment later it reappeared

glistening with bile on the toe
of the nun's black shoe.

This food could not enter my body.
Why did Sister not understand

force was pointless? I didn't mind
the dry white wafer at mass.

This egg was not the same.

Return to Rabka

The phone book is one-third full of our grandfather's name but
my cousin and I don't speak Polish, so can't look anyone up.
Maybe just as well. Since our grandparents left, it's been more
than a hundred years. The pretty town is split by a river and
nestled in mountains south of Krakow. It's famous for mineral
springs, year-round resorts, and medical spas, especially
for children.

There are still salt-works, where our grandmother worked
as a child. In another job, she wrapped rags on her feet
to polish the floors of well-off Jews. Back then, people said
shmatte katte zhid, which meant, "The Jew wipes his nose
on the dirty sleeve of his caftan." Poor Jews still wore caftans,
and their noses were always running. It took moving
to America to let one into the family. My cousin and
her parents always said they liked my father.

We walk by a park with a garden of rosebushes. They're
planted in a circle that proves to be a rosary. On Krakow
street corners, we saw people kneel to beg. I felt I'd been in
this city many times before. The Gorals, the mountain folk
we come from, were fond of music and flouting the law.
During Prohibition, our zither-playing grandfather boot-
legged in Minnesota. At the 16th century wooden church
where our grandparents were baptized, the family records
go back to 1780. Along the nave, the original frescoes
have lost most of their color. Red and blue traces of saints
and angels look ready to slide down the walls.

We stroll a street where Nazi police once shot babies tossed
into the air. It was part of their training. I read later
of the special school, now closed, for learning how to
implement the Final Solution in Poland. Local police
were pressed into service. We pass another school, still open,
where nuns hid children. We stop for soup and pierogi.
Poppyseed cake like Grandma made.

My cousin is still upset by Auschwitz. I was surprised
it seemed over-familiar, wished I hadn't seen *Schindler's
List*. But I can't forget the room of suitcases, the room
of hair. In Rabka, retaining walls hold pilfered Jewish
gravestones. The old Jewish graveyard is open but deserted.
In the Polish cemeteries, the graves are covered with fresh
flowers, and many of the headstones bear our family name.
On All Saints Day, people bring food to share with their dead.
Glass-covered candles burn all night to guide souls home.

At dinner, we drink too much vodka. My cousin asks if I
was raised Jewish. Did she forget my First Communion photos?
She doesn't know Jews were in Poland before it was Poland,
when the White God of Summer and the Black Goddess of Winter
ruled these hills, and the witch Jezi Baba took to the sky
in her mortar and pestle. All these wooden houses look like
they were designed by her. Same for those twisted haystacks
in the fields.

In the morning, hungover and alone, I hike the popular trail
to Morskie Oko. A mountain lake in the Tatras, its name means
Eye of the Sea. I keep thinking Eye of God, as nuns in habits
pass me. Surrounded by thousand-meter peaks, the Eye is steel
gray, set in a socket of stone. I feel the eyes of ghosts gazing
upon its shores. Of Jezi Baba, who led spirits through the forest.
She helped the pure of heart and ate the souls of the unclean.
Protected her home with a fence of human skulls and bones.
Swept away her tracks with a broom of human hair.

Double in the House of the Lord

Growing up split,
half-half, to whom
did I belong?

The math of genes
is easy: Simply divide
to multiply, but
cultural math
confounds.

My two halves
did not make a whole,
more like a double
of nothing.

Only one thing was certain:
I was a daughter of Eve.

Newcomers

The only Jews in town, my father's family
was respected. The churchgoers
in Red Oak, Iowa, considered them
People of the Book they hadn't read.

Kindergarten was a huge surprise,
a place where everyone spoke
another language and no one
understood my father's.

By the time a boy on the playground
told him the Jews killed Christ,
my father knew enough English
to ask, "Who's that?"

I don't know if his parents, Yiddish
speaking atheists from Odessa, provided
an answer to his question. In 1916,
America was at peace, little boys

in Red Oak could still watch horses
pull a fire engine through the streets, and,
as People of the Book, my grandparents
might have felt safe there from pogroms.

Origin Story

I'd like to have seen my grandfather's shop
in Oakland, lit up from outside
by street lamps when night
fell early in winter. He was closed
on *kratsmach,* the day
Jews had to scratch a living
while customers stayed
home for Christmas.
It took an educated eye
to buy and sell antiques
as he learned to do. Falling
asleep, I wish I could hear
his voice again,
which I can't remember,
can barely remember his face, only
his presence. I woke as a child
this morning, my disordered
bed warm with body traces.
My past changes without me,
an empty house
that continues to weather.
No one knew where
my grandfather came from,
if he was born
in Warsaw or Odessa.
An orphan is on his own.
His past changes too, now,
long after he might have told me
to pay attention if
I don't want to miss the details.

Deus Absconditus

Jesus looks at me from his cross and I suddenly know: He's only
human. He says my name. Heaven has changed, but our
second-grade nun didn't hear. She keeps reading aloud,
preparing the class for First Holy Communion.

My mother throws a coat over her nightgown to drive me
to mass, then waits in the car with a book. My father's Jewish.
They're both atheists.

If I could go outside, I might see God as an almost-face
in a cloud. And feel the warm breath of the Holy Ghost.
Those two like being invisible. When I asked why, Sister said,
It's a mystery.

I stare at Jesus. He stays silent. What if he came down?
I could wipe the blood from his hands, comb his matted hair.
We could go for a walk. I would share my sandwich.

Jesus looks like he's thinking it over. But he doesn't move.
How am I supposed to live the rest of my life?

A priest comes in, points to a water stain under the crucifix
tells us it looks like Golgotha. I see a dingy wall and feel
embarrassed by the show. God deserves more.
Yet I need to be kind.

Certainty ends, longing begins. Many years later I learn
that when Pompey conquered Jerusalem, drove his chariot
through streets of golden stone, he entered the Holy of Holies,
the Temple's most sacred space, and was amazed
to find it was an empty room.

Broken Family

After I learned that Jesus was a Jew
and Jews and Christians didn't get along,
I wondered how that felt to him.
Up in heaven, he seemed content
but, like me, might feel adrift,
as if he didn't quite fit in.

On Earth, Jesus lay in our basement,
one of many shining figures
handed down to but ignored
by my parents. Yet he still belonged
to dad's people as well as mom's
and, like a kid after a divorce,
I longed to reunite my family.

I wanted to invite them all,
holy and human, living and dead,
to dinner with me and my folks.
But there'd be no sitting down together.
There was no longer even a table.

I could only herd random angels
left to roam like pets becoming feral
on abandoned property.

Born of Polish Women

Our world, a long gray river contained
by an overturned basin of sky,
a single pewter cloud. Yet
within the house find
the snow-white-red
embroidered softness
of our Christmas
dinner napkin,
a joyous bosom, sprouting
winter berries.
Christ's blood
flows toward us
all the year as we
kneel in churches
where no lady-breast will spill
wine upon the altar clothing,
no milk is served at mass.

Untouched and Untouchable

That's how your best friend describes you,
in a letter I find in your vanity after death.
I am agog at her words as if they'd been written
for me, a prediction that I too would feel
this way about you. I remember your touch,
awkward and a little rough as you pulled
a brush through my hair, scrubbed milk
from my mouth before sending me off
in my green pleated skirt to brusque nuns.
Today I must go through your clothes.

I walk into your closet where after school
I loved to handle your open-toe suede heels
that so glamorously concealed your bunions.
Here I draw my fingers through the ridges
of a pink chenille robe you wore to feed me
a bottle. You hoarded your breasts, but later
let me stare at their long dark nipples
while you lay in a bath. They floated
above the water and when they grew cold,
you draped them with warm, wet washcloths.
Your face relaxed, and I felt alone.

I never knew what was in your fine mind,
that icy knife passed down to you
through a thousand Polish winters, only
that it bent and sharpened by the year.
I learned to flinch when you shot out a hand
to push back my bangs. Now I press my face
into leopard-skin blouses still silently firing
your scent, and all that you left untouched
in me lies in my chest, untouchable.

Entertaining the Troops
(for my mother)

by day she was only a clerk
in the shipyard office

no Rosie showing off
feminine strength   riveting steel

for her the thrill came on Saturday night
dancing with sailors in need

of company   hopefully fast
before shipping out

far away a world dying
here   excitement

men going
maybe not coming back

The Big Band played
for as long as it takes to fall in love

song after song she felt
each partner's body

shoulder bones covered
by big soft collars

inside bell bottom
trousers   mini-cannons

holding fire
on her rayon-clad, married hip

all the men safe
for as long as she could hold them

Exhibit A

We were too young to know
that the soft shape hanging

between his legs could shift
leave his body to fly

all by itself
out of our house and land

like something carved
from the divine

one of those phalluses
erected on every street corner

in ancient Greek towns
or sold to tourists in Bhutan.

Confronted with our father's
dangling display

what was a little girl
to think?

My sister thought better
than to worship false idols

of which this was her first.
Pointed the other way

I strolled to the pagan church.

Eve Departs

Passing the tree, she approaches the gate.
Adam runs to catch up.
What is she doing? he asks.
The animals gather, wait for her answer.
Something is missing, she thinks.
But all that she needs is here.
And the Father loves her. He does.
In an almost unconditional way.
But she's not sure He understands her.

The angels draw closer. All are waiting,
the beasts of the field, the birds
of the sky, the sea creatures.
The female animals in particular
are listening. The mouse, the lion,
the wife of the snake.
Understanding breaks an egg,
spills the yolk.
She needs to leave to find her mother.

Scorched Milk

After Paradise came mother's milk,
taste of survival laced with bliss,
and after that, cooking. Substitutes
are tricky. Cow's milk can mix
with butter and flower for béchamel,
and also eggs and sugar, for cake
and custard. But it can't be browned
as in *beurre noisette*, a roux
for ragout, caramel. Unless as part
of an Indian sweet, it resists
overheating, being pushed.
Left alone in a covered pot
it becomes hypersensitive.
Unlike water, it must be watched
with loving kindness lest it boil
and burn with an odorous ardor
from which there is no going back.
The cook must add vinegar and baking
soda, or lemon and salt, scrub like
a scullery slave, to clean the taste of scorch.

The cook can also try Wiener Mix-up, in this recipe
from the 1950s:

Take 1lb. frankfurters, thinly sliced, cans of chopped ripe olives,
whole kernel corn, and cut string beans, 1 cup diced cheddar
cheese, 2 cups tomato catsup, sugar, salt, garlic salt, and one
small onion, finely chopped. Mix all together, turn into a
casserole dish and bake, covered, in a moderate oven
for an hour. Serves 6-8.

Climbing the Tree of Life

I named my grandmothers for the color
of their hair. White Grandma was Catholic,
scary, and strict, like the Holy Church.
Black Grandma was Jewish and brown
like the earth in her garden and the eggplant
salad she kept in her fridge. The godless
Jewish relatives were all snappy and funny
and smart. Intellectuals, activists, artists.
I wanted to be like them but wasn't sure
I could measure up, couldn't tell where
I stood with people who were always kidding.
The Catholics were smart too but never as funny.
They served in the military, looked me
straight in the eye, didn't talk over my head.
They had big jobs and cabins in the woods,
lakes, and the aurora borealis. They drank
whiskey, filled their freezers with venison.
The Jewish houses had pianos and violins
that got played a lot, were full of books
that got discussed. They read Andre Schwarz-Bart's
The Last of the Just. The Catholics read
James Michener's *Hawaii*. They loved to read,
but didn't have libraries. They subscribed
to *Catholic Digest* and never missed mass,
which made me glad they lived in other states.
Except for cute altar boys, I couldn't wait
for mass to end. I wondered why Jesus and Mary
had to be so holy. I wanted Jesus to be sexy.
My relatives were part of me and I of them.
I had my favorites, but there was no
understanding anything. My hands
and fingernails with their long beds
looked just like my mother's, my square toenails
like my father's. Once, when Uncle Louis
and I were barefoot at a pool, I was shocked
to see we had the same short toes.

Memento Mori

The afternoon my grandmother died
my father took me with him
to the hospital. He kissed her good-bye
on her cheek, and I couldn't,
in case it was cold. That night
I dreamed of skeletons
lying in graves, losing flesh.

But they keep their eyebrows,
my father said, as he fried bacon.
What's more, they wiggle
them when they come out at night
to dance. He wiggled his, and I saw
my grandmother's—black, bushy, and
often raised, when something was funny.

Later I saw skulls in the hundreds,
skeletons wearing fancy dress.
In the Capuchin crypts, on Mexico's
Day of the Dead, bones showed how
to connect and persist. But that morning,
over breakfast, was the first time
they made me laugh.

Learning to See through Atheist Eyes

Senator McCarthy was on TV, and my father wore
his Adlai Stevenson shoe-with-a-hole-in-it pin.
In another must-watch show, Elizabeth wore ermine
and white satin to be crowned Queen of England.

I saw that one with my mother, who bought
me my own white-satin, pearl-studded dress
to make First Communion. Elizabeth felt blessed
by God, believed in her divine responsibility to serve.
Jesus belonged to my father's tribe, so wasn't really
God, but I swallowed him anyway.

Later, someone stuck *under God* into the Pledge
of Allegiance. Like my parents, I disapproved.
When my 4th-grade class reached those words,
I chose to remain silent. It was worse for Uncle Louis
who had to hide for a week at Clear Lake.
He never became a citizen, and if he answered
the government's subpoena, might be deported.
All the way back to Russia where he started.

After Confirmation, I stopped going to church.
Uncle Louis was never found out, and
Clear Lake's blue-green algae is now
so plentiful it can be seen from outer space.

Summer Vacations at Clear Lake

Cherries ran rampant
on those mother-and-daughter
sundresses you bought for us
to wear at the lake. You, my sister,
and I, all dressed alike.

When we reached the float,
my sister and I stripped off
our dresses. We wore bathing
suits beneath and couldn't wait
to swim. You could only dog-paddle,
never put your head under water.
You'd get in later, after reading
your book a while. Before dinner,
you might make a fruit pie.

You'd tell us about your parents' truck farm
where you picked strawberries
with your sisters. All there was
for lunch in summer, with fresh milk.
Your family was poor but healthy,
survived the Spanish flu with help
from your mother's blackberry cordial.
You wore your sisters' hand-me-down
dresses all year, and in winter,
the same pair of socks until
they stood up by themselves.

Summer was the only time
we wore mother-and-daughter
dresses. As if that were their season,
along with cherries, a firm fruit
that lasted longer than berries.

My Cousin and I Hunted Salamanders

I endured the touch of their shiny, maroon-
colored bodies, the way their feather feet tickled
as they lifted them to drag their moist bellies
and lizard tails across my palm. As I waited
for my cousin to get them off me, they would halt,
push themselves up on short arms, raise
their broad-snouted heads. He was fearless,
a boy who loved everything that lived outside,
learned the names and habits of every insect,
animal, and plant in our garden. Picking up rocks,
he uncovered salamanders breathing
through their skins in wet soil, as many
as he could. When we were done, he replaced
them exactly where he found them.
Back inside, we washed our hands
before trading clothes with each other.
Two years older and taller by a foot, my cousin
was gracious, didn't complain as my dress
strained across his chest, revealed his naked knees.
His shirtsleeves hung far over my wrists, his pants
nearly slid off my hips, and I was thrilled
as our parents reviewed us. We paraded cool
as salamanders who can poison, put out
a fire or survive one. After college, we exchanged
only letters, which my cousin had to write
in pencil on yellow, ruled paper. He was in prison
for molesting boys, and some of his words
got inked out by the censor. But not
when he wrote, *Isn't it ironic? I grew up*
to be the perv, yet cross-dressing came first
and was your idea. I remembered longing
for nature to transform me, while he
only wanted to know its creatures better,
a desire that somehow led to fires so terrible
even a salamander could not live through them.

Gender Confusion

I had it, all right. Father with symbolic
breasts, mother with symbolic penis.

What did my therapist mean? Merely
that he was the more nurturing one,

she the mean boss. The theoretical
lens didn't matter. But breasts

could turn hard, mountains tipped
with nipples of granite, and a penis

could be friendly as a puppy.
There were too many phallic

symbols to list. And so obvious.
All those weapons and monuments.

But yonic? The shell, the lotus,
the gaping wound of Christ.

It was confusing.

Indefensible

When our father wore only a white
sleeveless undershirt and roamed
insouciant through our home
my younger sister used to shout,
Wear pants!

Our mother shrugged, and I, his ally,
grinned as he joked,
*If you see something God
didn't make, throw a stick at it!*

Always at eye level, my youngest
sister later recalled.

My outraged sister said, *Come on.*
You must have felt shame.
Not that I knew of.

I wanted to be a burlesque dancer,
have ten children by ten men,
travel the globe, join the merchant
marines, be the favorite of the sultan.

I wanted to be free, and didn't know
what God had to do with it. Unless
the revelations of the flesh.

Touring Topkapi Harem You Imagine

Here is where you were born and
Mother picks the concubines.
Most are imported, but, like you,
many emerge in these quarters.
Mother controls the vast family, grows
the bureaucracy. Watch out, she has eyes
in the walls, ears everywhere.

The palace is beautiful, lavish,
but smaller as you realize
you have grown up confined
to these rooms you can't leave.
Like the blue-and-green plants
whose patterns cover the walls,
your life here changes
only to repeat, while you wait.

Far below, boats cross the Bosporus.
If you could reach it, you'd sail
back and forth, east side to west side,
farther, beyond the channel, to one sea
or another, the world. You would strip
off your clothes and put on a sailor's,
stoke the boiler, hoist the jib, watch
dark water curl under stars. But it's time
for tea in another tiled room.

The Extra Leg

My sister and I leafed through photos
of nature's mistakes
in our father's medical book
to find our favorite, the leg
growing out of a man's back.
We understood—this leg
could not be fixed. It was designed to go
the wrong way. Its knee was bent,
and its foot faced the floor
but couldn't reach it. Not without pulling
the man over backward,
making him fall
and maybe not then.
This was a leg ready to walk
that could not take a step.
The same size as the man's
other legs, it looked healthy.
It didn't know
two more were behind it,
or the man,
looking the other way.

Kidnapped Girls

One is not born, but rather becomes, a woman.
—Simone de Beauvoir, *The Second Sex*

Yeah, but some things we seem almost born knowing, don't we?
Like our knowing to follow those first-grade Oakland boys
who knew to take us, their girl classmates and neighbors,
straight up our hilly block to an abandoned shack
in an empty field. The shack was just across the street
from one boy's house, where a mother was at home,
but still seemed far away and kind of dangerous
once they got us in there. Those boys also knew to order us
to take down our pants, and we knew to comply and act
like prisoners though we knew this wasn't really real—
nobody made a fist or even touched us—which made me feel
a little silly. Then the boys ran out of ideas, got bored,
and our whole gang drifted away.

Things were different when my grandmother was visiting.
On another kidnapping afternoon, who knows how, she knew
to suddenly loom, huge and backlit, at the head of an alley
two doors from my house. We girls had been abducted
only moments before, and the boys were busy showing us
theirs if we showed them ours. Everything seemed okay until
the dark figure that was Grandma started cawing
like a giant crow as she bawled us out and everyone ran.
Where is she now that she's needed, in Oakland and everywhere
slavers have grown into their knowing?

They're getting away with it, Grandma, but I'd like to think
this nonsense never could have happened on your watch. O, my stern
Grandma, who stood so firmly against any illegal, impure,
and dangerous forms of sex (you knew all sex was dangerous
to women), how I would rejoice to hear you caw again,
your voice gathering power like an unbearable siren
heard by everyone on Earth, until it could finally disperse
all bad boys grown old, from girls who can no longer escape.

Minnesota Christmas

I don't remember which cousins invited me
up into the hayloft in their freezing barn.
Jump, they urged, and I flew back down
onto a pile of dusty hay, stood up exhilarated
until I felt the unexpected heat
of blood dropping from my nose.
I remember tiny Great-aunt Cele,
who silently handed me her handkerchief
and inexplicably showed me her chest,
opening her blouse a bit to reveal
a bare plank with two knotholes
where her breasts had been.
Did she know that at twelve,
I was a woman myself?
A month ago, first thinking
the rusty stain I spied
was somehow shit,
I'd quickly figured out—
only lying on the bathroom floor,
naked belly pressing onto tiles,
could chill the brand-new pain of cramps.

She's very ethereal, I later overheard
Cele tell the family, and I was, my every airy part
a mystery waiting to spark.
I knew nothing but was ready
for whatever came, a summer
when I'd feel those words
from *Peyton Place* I'd memorized
burn real, like Betty in short-shorts
when Rodney's hand "found the V of her crotch."
Those red-hot words were borrowed from me
on that visit, though not by Cele,
who never wed, lived all her life
on the farm with her married sister,

a cousin told me when we too were old.
She was like a living saint, he said,
worked so hard every day, tried to please
them all and never complained
except for once in a while
a long sigh ending in oh pshaw.

That Christmas, years past surgery,
two years before her end,
her virgin eggs, like mine now, gone,
Cele noticed me, not what I carried.
It was my mother and her sisters,
readers all, who couldn't resist
sneaking a look at the scandalous,
just-published paperback book
winking from my nightstand.

Each night I found deepening dog-ears
stroked by matronly fingers.
I was the youngest woman there
but the uncontested owner
of that blistering paper,
just as I owned my blood,
my triple A breasts,
and my new red-wool Italian sweater
from Marshall Field's, a gift
from my wealthiest aunt.
The entire family, except my Jewish dad,
might have gone to midnight mass,
but I only remember standing up
with the women, wearing my
medieval-style sweater like a blazon,
as we sang with conviction:
Joy to the World!

Nativity Tales

Jewish Midwives:

We women heard a story so sad, so strange—about a young
mother-to-be. She'd just come of age when told from on high,
like old Sarah before her, of a miracle son she'd conceive.
Her angel departed, and, when her time came, she was forced
to travel, without mother, sisters, or any other female kin,
with only a husband, who was not her child's father. The Lord
sent a star as a guide, but to a town that held nothing
she needed; not one room, one woman like us to help her,
with warm, oiled hands, and a voice, to tell her, *Push,
you and your boy will live*. She had only that untrained man,
an ass and some cows, all silently watching that star's silent
light shine down till baby was come. A while later three more
men brought gifts: costly, magnificent, nothing they needed.

Mary:

No one ever asked, so I never told, but for the record,
I did not bring forth in pain like other women,
nor was I helpless in that stable. Only the Star
that watched over me knows: the Holy Ghost
was my midwife, and God my partner on the ride.
Fused into one, we surfed tsunamis, shot
through volcanoes, sang praise with all Earth's flowers.
We entered the Sun's holy center as pilgrims
and loved, until God Our Father was ready
to bring Himself forth as Our Son
and shine in my arms. It was all joy; the pain
came later, and after that, Heaven.

First Purchase

The family stopped at a roadside stand
somewhere in the hot, dusty West,
and I picked out a rose and gold ring.
The first jewelry I chose
for myself was nothing special
yet magical. I hadn't known gold
could come in two colors, braided
in two twisting strands. How delicate
the rose would look. Someone
had discovered these properties
and woven them into a circle
I could wear the rest of my life
if I didn't lose it. Near the register,
my mother slipped me some cash.
Back in the car, my father took
the wheel again and barreled
past more sage and cacti. She
looked out toward distant mesas,
and I sat behind them, lost
in the landscape I saw on my finger.

If a Tree Were Your Mother

A friend told me she climbed a redwood
in her backyard every day to escape from her mother.
Sometimes she'd strap herself to it right at the top
and sleep there all night. She said, *Once I fell seventy-five feet*
all the way to the ground, but the branches broke
my fall and I wasn't even hurt. What if your mother

were that tree, an ever-red, evergreen
redwood, living thousands of years
with a lineage going back millions, laughing at gravity
while raising dark earth-matter to light, wore a necklace
of ferns and shrubs, drank a swimming pool's worth of fog
to water herself at dawn, could drop a new family
in fairy rings at her feet, sprout new trees from her sides
after illness or cutting, resurrect from her roots after fire;
if your mother were the oldest, tallest, longest-lived,
able to save you with her hundred arms from falling,
what could you not do with your life?

II. Dangers

Visiting the Old Neighborhood

Have you come for your spanking?
he asked as he opened the door.
His smile was knowing.

When I lived next-door, one of his sons
and I were sweethearts, got married
in their big backyard. I wore a dishrag veil.

Neighborhood kids were the guests.
Sometimes we all met in my basement,
explored one another. I thought this was secret.

He looked the same, though I'd never seen
him this close. Back then he mowed
the lawn. The mom was nice, let us lick
leftover cake batter from the bowl.

After dinner all seven of them knelt
in the living room to say the rosary.
I didn't come over then.

What did he mean by my *spanking*?
He waited and his smile said he knew.
I was dirty and didn't have an answer.

Getting Away

When the detective rang our bell, told us we once lived next-door
to the killer, I was excited. Mom, Dad, and I
were part of the Berkeley murder. Burton Abbott's face
was in the paper every day, looking blank,
not dangerous. I read how Stephanie disappeared
walking home from junior high, her French book
got tossed in the hills above the bay, her bra
buried in his backyard. I was in grade school,
still wore a white undershirt; he might have driven
right by. Long ago when we were neighbors,
had he noticed the toddler running away on her trike?
My parents claimed I gave them the slip,
and I could remember the sheer joy of pedaling.
She's fast, gone to the park to pick up sailors,
went the family joke. No one could catch me
but, sometimes, went the story, a neighbor's yellow dog
dragged me back by my sleeve. Now they told the detective
we'd never met the killer. I was glad
when bloodhounds finally found the body. Soon
he would be gassed.

Later, when it was cool to hitchhike,
I didn't really look at who was driving me to Berkeley—
until he smiled and drew his gun.
I said, *You're kidding*, as he stopped for a light.
Time shrank to an O the size of the barrel.
I stared down it, glanced at his eyes. Impossible
to tell what he was thinking. But he was small,
bland, and skinny, just like Abbott, and I thought I'd rather die
right there than go with him to slow death
in the hills. I turned my back, opened the door
and slid out. Forced my legs to walk.
When his car pulled ahead and vanished
around the corner, I felt the thrill
of the pleasures we had exchanged,
his, when he thought he had me,
mine, when I got away.

Understood

In 1939, as Hitler invaded Poland,
my parents' marriage in Reno was legal
but almost interracial. Jews were not yet white
in America. My grandma told my mother,
I never thought you'd marry one.
It was a crime under Franz Joseph.

At home, my parents didn't talk about the Jews
missing from Europe. At my Catholic school,
the Jews killed Jesus.

After we saw "The Diary of Anne Frank,"
my Commie aunt told her son, *She
wouldn't understand.* She told me
what I already knew: *You can't be a Jew
without a Jewish mother.* Mom and I
were *shiksas.*

An Irish-Catholic boyfriend's aunt, a nun,
came for Christmas dinner and asked,
Like my new coat? I got it cheap, in Jew-town.
For Crypto-Jews, the Inquisition wasn't over.

Soon enough, I understood. The Jews
might reject but wouldn't kill me.
With anyone else, I couldn't be certain.

Eating Figs in a Field Between Ranch Houses

My mother and I crunch through thin,
gray-green skin to pinkish-
orange flesh. It's not stealing
if we eat where we stand.

As usual, we don't talk
about anything important,
or touch. I wish we could be soft
and giving as figs in October.

Apple and peach trees
blossom like brides
before bearing fruit.
The luscious fig differs.

We're feasting on sweet
remains, of female flowers
that grew unseen, trapped
inside the fruit they became.

Red Light, Green Light

Whoever played it can't forget
that childhood game. Of running,
stopping, waiting like a statue,
sometimes wobbling on one leg,
to run again, straight ahead,
one light at a time.

In a car, it's impossible to drive
with one foot on the brake
but worse to accidentally hit
the gas and crash. It's even worse
if you're in reverse. Opposing lights
should not be on at the same time.

In families, seed can be turned,
made to run backward, away
from life, instead of straight ahead.
The stopped children can't forget.
Red light, green light, both on
at the same time, burning
the eye like something nuclear.

Flash-Frozen

Alone in bed at night
a girl curled up
tight as a pillbug
I stowed away
inside Flash Gordon's rocket
waited to be loved
or banished to some desert
planet where I'd screech
with witches till I slept,
near armadillos in a dry defile.

Lying with my lawful mate
I am again the child
whose vision, like a fly's,
is mosaic, sees everything
about the parts but how
they fit together.
In some seasons
we might as well be crew
from Shackleton's ship
stuck in Antarctic ice.

Report by Detective Alma Robado

The victim said her soul was kidnapped
but she didn't see a face or hear a voice

so couldn't provide a description, or ID
suspects in a lineup. She couldn't pay

a ransom, because no one ever called.
She only knew where she was when

it was taken and what was happening
before it disappeared, along with that thief

in the deep night that descended on her
days and left her in the world alone.

After so many years, she didn't know where
or how to look but had always sensed

her soul was close, yet so well hidden
she might never find it.

It was the kind of case we see too often.
With no leads, and against our advice,

she began a thorough search on her own,
and would not give up. She was sure

if she did, the case would get even colder.
Nothing was more important, and apart

from her investigation, she ignored a lot else
she needed to do to stay alive

which only made her life more dangerous.
She didn't care. Without her soul, she said,

there was nothing more to lose. And
she didn't want to die until she found it,

if she ever did. She wanted to ask her soul
just where in hell it had been

all this time, even if it couldn't answer.

Visiting the Convent at San Marco

I want to live in one of its cells,
with a bed, desk, and Fra Angelico
fresco, a pink annunciation afloat
on plaster. As a child I laid rocks
on the grass in the backyard,
to mark a rectangular space
meant for me alone. Stepping
inside it, I saw the back of my house
where I didn't want to be. At the end
of the yard I'd once seen a robin
with a ripped-open gut
lined with three rosy worms.
If this was a building with roof and walls
it could keep things out or let them in.
A home kept out strangers, a church
let in God. I hadn't heard
of open-air temples, the world
as holy home, *beit ha kodesh*.
I loved feeling safe inside
this open frame. Now,
leaving the monk's cell, I visit
the rest of the frescoed rooms
along the hall, peer through interior
windows at the cloister garden. Turning
the corner, I find the cell reserved
for the convent's Medici patron
and the one for Savonarola, until
the rebel was hanged and burned
in a city square. I am amazed to see
his black, hooded cloak has survived.
Displayed freestanding in the center
of the room, the raven breathes.

Next Step

One afternoon I walked a concrete ledge
that ran below the windows of an office
where I had a summer job. All day I transcribed
legal documents from a tape recorder
onto five sheets of typing paper, each one
separated from the next by a thin
layer of carbon paper, to make corrections
easier on the green Selectric typewriter.

After lunch, I climbed out a window,
stood on the ledge, faced the street
fourteen stories below. With my back
to the window, the ledge seemed wide
enough. I turned sideways, calculated
the distance between the beginning
of the next, closed, window, and its end,
about four feet. To get there and back
I'd have to put one foot in front of the other,
surely, not too fast, and stay calm
to keep my balance, especially
on the turn. It was a sunny day.
I thought I could do it.

It was only afterward that I felt
the toss of my coin, the flip
of fear in my gut. I didn't usually test
my courage, didn't drive too fast,
backpack alone. I wouldn't dive
from the high board, tried to avoid
rapists and bears. I wasn't suicidal,
or pregnant, couldn't be drafted.
Just living was enough of a risk.

Into the Woods

Once when a friend and I were out in the woods,
stoned on LSD, we saw a man looking at us
as he played with himself, and discussed
how we should react. I'm trying not to laugh,
I whispered. My friend asked whether
we should say something to him.

I wasn't afraid, because the man
was on the other side of a wide creek
and my friend was also a man.
A woman and a man, really high,
we looked at the other man showing us
his goods and could not think what to do.

In patriarchy, it's said, what a woman
fears most from a man is being hurt,
while what he most fears from her
is being laughed at. It's said that a man
is either a woman's rapist or her defender.
These two men were neither.

My friend and I couldn't stop looking
at that bird-in-the-hand, as it asked
to be appreciated, and seemed delighted
to be noticed, from a safe distance.
Freud said civilization began with upright
posture, which made genitals visible.

Appetite

Spending the night with my sister, I wake to a moan.
Help, help, sounds from her room. Then silence.

Only a dream, but next morning, she glowers.
She can't remember calling out, yet insists
I should have rushed in. She was crying, *Save me!*

I lie on her couch and feel a bland smoothness,
something hard and neutral encase me, as if in Styrofoam.

As a colicky baby my screams once got so bad
our father could only watch as our mother
held me straight out from her chest
like a suspect package. Their firstborn,
past consoling. Was this the start of my disconnect?

We need breakfast. I could make us fresh-squeezed
orange juice and "gentle eggs," scrambled
super-slow with lots of butter and tarragon,
the way my sister taught me. I'm afraid
asking will only feed her rage.

Being Treated as Dead

How tribal it feels, like being shunned
by Amish, shown the dirt
road out from a Pilgrim town,
forbidden to place a last offering

of flowers in a palm leaf
basket at the village shrine
in Bali. But even a family
of two sisters is a tribe.

A radioactive horse between us
couldn't decay fast enough
for us to outlive its halflives.
She disowned me, left me

for dead, like a daughter
of Orthodox Jews who marries
a goy. Did she sit shiva,
cover mirrors? Does she light

yahrzeit candles? I'm wearing
a shroud, so can't understand
how she can still send cards
for Christmas and my birthday,

containing still more cards entitling
me to free coffee. Is she buying
time? Will I be dead only for
a decade, like an ostracized

Athenian official? If life,
as a Buddhist teacher said,
boils down to three words,
not always so, do I try to detach

from both hope and fear?
I feel like Schrödinger's cat,
condemned to remain
both dead and alive, or half

of an entangled pair of sub-atomic
particles that can't unknow each other,
from any distance. After thirty
years of not speaking

to her sister, our dying
mother said, *This is silly*
I should call her, but didn't.
Constellations revolve, above

and below the horizon.
Tracked by stars, malign
and kind—before death,
who can say what's final?

Early Accounting

I am hardly a whore
my mother agrees

when I say I take love
not cash.

Then she adds
I have yet to be loved

for no man has given
me his fortune.

I don't say that she
has been fortunate

her husband
has loved like a child

who learns to forget
the need for a good return.

That the good wife reconciles
love with gold

when both are his. Or
that the children are killed

in the secret
marriage of the courtesan.

Follower

Call me crazy, I loved a mad man
who offered me a way to live. I couldn't find
another way and jumped into his caravan. He
might have been a con man. He parked
at the edge of the desert pit I'd crawled
out of and didn't want to fall back in.
He saw salvation ahead, I feared
apocalypse. We circled the pit's rim.
I thought I might have invented him,
wasn't sure he knew I was there.
Sometimes he sounded like Moses,
at other times Don Quixote.
His was the pure word
upon word and it didn't matter
if I heard it. What mattered
was to get a driver, find some way
for the Dead Sea not to sink entirely,
leaving nothing but a cold light
on our planet and only red-hot
memories of neon, a noble gas
whose name means new.

When the Minotaur Was a Girl

—Ariadne returns for her half-sister.

Greetings, Ariadne. Tell the truth. If I'd been all-girl, slim
and pretty like you, would you have helped him try
to murder me?

You're breathing? You're still alive?

You woke me from a nap.

Impossible.

I'm surprised to see you too. You traded my life for a promise
of marriage. What kind of sister does that?

Theseus told me you were dead when he left this chamber.
Was that another lie? Like when he said he loved me?

He thought he finished me. Look at the scar on my neck.

Huge. Still, how lovely your woman's head looks, so like our mother's.
Yet so small atop your father's gift to you, your godlike bull's body.

Oh yes, I'm a real family monster. Another reason to get rid
of me.

Poor, cursed thing, if only you'd turned out part cow. Instead
of locking you away, we could have kept you in my garden,
fed you grass.

No need for regrets. The young humans were tasty.

You must believe this, after Theseus abandoned me, I flew
into a fury. Then thought of you and was ashamed. I wished
only to return, give you a proper burial.

So finally, you understand rage. I'm not impressed.

Sister, I beg you to forgive me. I loved that man as much
as I feared your awful hunger.

I'm hungry now. Why don't you feed me those funeral offerings? I'd like to try that honey and wine.

Of course. Open your mouth. And please, watch where you step.

Delicious. I'll have another cup.

Now, Sister, you must let me help: I have a new man now, a god who is my husband. Come with me.

To live in your yard like a pet?

You'll live like a queen in our palace. You can't stay here. Outside this room, the walls have collapsed.

I brought them down after Theseus left.

All by yourself? Zeus help me! Well, it's hot out there. I'll give you my hat.

How about a dress, to cover my animal parts?

What nonsense. You're splendid just as you are. I'd be thrilled to have your strength.

You don't need it, not with your looks.

Please. We can walk away and be immortals.

As a woman-beast? No thanks.

We can be happy together. Trust me; I've changed so much.

You're still a princess. And so stupid.

I'm still your sister.

So let me tell you: I could have killed your darling warrior in a minute. But I hoped if I let him go, you people would leave me alone. Is there any more food?

You're still hungry?

You have no idea how much I can eat. If I were you, I'd go now.

Flawed Feminist

Girlfriends, you've asked—

if I wanted a man to take care of me.

I understand your question. You're not all
feminists, but your mothers were strong,
came from pioneer stock. They were not anxious
or clinically depressed. Not one of them needed
a man to take care of her, nor, I'm guessing,
did their mothers before them. Not for hundreds of years.

I don't know why you keep your own men around.
I only question:

Do they know they're on probation?

I wanted to be an artist but didn't quite dare.
Like my mother, I was a flâneur. My inborn rhythm
was that of a beachcomber. But dollar bills
can rarely be gathered from the shore.

I fell in love with a man whose big dream
required a golden goose, not a pigeon like me.

He felt like fate. I bet my life.

Girlfriends—

Do you remember ever
feeling something like this?

I only wanted to go on the ride
and even after our very long drive
on mountain roads with potholes
and drop-off sides
I'm there—
for the teenage thrill, the dream.

Violence Against Women

It's in the blood
        that pops up penis-golems
                dumb messengers of death and doom

 in flood that monthly bears away
        your unraped egg
                dead as its army of micro-suitors

or bathes
        the living, growing child
            whose birth can kill you

Urgent blood
        lies in wait
            on the stairs, in the woods, in the alley

makes you wait
        for its pound on house or car

doors locked   both hands on the wheel
        can't be too careful

you're driving
        but it's breathing
            inside you

Cow of Plenty

My youngest sister adored cows, but I didn't understand
the attraction. She found music in their lowing,
tenderness in their gaze. As we hiked
past a herd, keeping our distance
so we wouldn't spook them, or get between
any calf and its mother, she'd say,
I cherish those faces. I felt uneasy,
as if their blankness might be hiding
angry spirits. She saw pure love
look back from their hypnotic eyes.
I knew what she craved the morning
she told me, *If you really cared,*
last night you would have picked me up,
given me your bed. I'd do it for you,
if your mind was scrambled eggs.
By then she'd been bucking for years,
felt weakened, like a bull slashed
by *picadors* and *banderilleros.*
She was sick of her husband, weary
of psych wards like bad motels
with stale chips and no ice. After concerts,
she drove home alone in her orchestra
dress, her handmade viola locked
in the trunk of her red, two-seater.
There were times she pulled over, waded
into the black evening ocean,
up to her neck. She said, *If I had money,*
I'd get the best shrink on earth. I thought
she needed one like Kamadehnu,
the divine cow who gives all she has,
unlike our mother, who threatened
over Cheerios she might not be around
when her child got home from school.
The day my sister drove in pre-dawn darkness
to her death, her husband suffered

only a hairline crack to his clavicle,
yet couldn't remember what happened
before the crash. Did four hands fight
on the wheel? Did she swerve
toward a suit of lights, leap a fence?
The next time I stopped by cattle,
I watched them eat in silence
and thought about being a cow
so hard I slipped inside one.
I stood, solid as a truck,
then lowered my head, bowing
all the way down to the earth
to receive its grass. I've never nursed,
but I could feel the tug of milk.

Blood Diamond

My sister and I were on the phone, retelling how our father
was paid in kind by an old-lady crook of a client
and came home with a marquise diamond, a long, pointed oval
gorgeously set in a platinum ring. The doll earned her gem
as a Teapot-Dome-Scandal doxy, boarded a train
in a silk-Georgette dress, carried papers from her man
to one of Harding's, the first Cabinet member to see prison.
And you're the first to hear this, she assured our father,
as he kept her from going to jail for a con decades later.
Still fetching and trim in a girdle, she settled her fee
with the marquise, a mink stole, and a cherry-red, '56 Caddy.

And are you wearing that diamond today? my sister asked.
Maybe she'd rather forget what happened next, how I begged
our mother to leave me the ring, and she promised, then gave
it to our youngest sister, who, when I told her I was hurt,
said *take it*, to which I said *no, you keep it*, but she died too,
in a freeway crash, so it wound up with our brother-in-law,
who said I could have it but lied.

I thought of the trail of deceptions that led to this ending,
beginning with mine. Telling myself the marquise meant love,
not carbon. Our sister's struggle to live with the man she married
mostly for money. Her husband asking our father
if he could inherit her share of our fortune and, hearing
he couldn't, taking off with the diamond. That ring
passed into and through our family, a jewel snaking
its way through the guts of a smuggler.

Case Closed

I'm closing the book on your sister, the therapist said,
after failing to save her client from death.

My sister had been the driver and no one could stop
her accident on the long highway.

The therapist had finally referred her
to the best shrink, and the right cocktail
of drugs had begun to work, but too late.

I'd failed too, and despised the woman I'd called,
for shutting me down and shutting me up.

In silence, I cursed her, ordered smoke
from my sister's cremation to find her
office door, smear it with a permanent mark.

An eye for an eye, a life for a life, vengeance
is a magic spell to replace what was lost.

Did the therapist feel the heat of my eye,
how it blazed to make her pay?

She couldn't wait to close her book, but I wanted
my grief fed.

I lit a signal fire on a cliff, with sky-high flames
that would let my sister find me.

In the Orchards of Eden

At an outdoor café, we sip margaritas,
and my oldest friend says she's done
with all that is dark. From now on
she wants only light. I know she's weary
of my darkness and weird fear
that too much radiance could pull
me from Earth before I'm ready.

Licking lime and salt from her palm,
she reassures me: *It's spiritual, not
personal. As girls we ate too many
dark fruits.* I hear her abandon me
along with the tree that fed us
and am scared to ask if we'll meet
again for a long birthday lunch.

Across the table, backlit by sun,
she's a shadow with a glowing edge.
I don't want to lose her. I want her
with me in the spoiled garden,
where light and dark are still a pair.

It's Over but Feels Like the Jury's Still Out

sequestered with old pizza
and transcripts from my trial

where time was the judge
my life the defendants and plaintiffs
I the lawyers and bailiff

a verdict was delivered
but not yet the sentence
for what came before

put me in the dock
as both prisoner and witness

of my not knowing
enough
then as now

It feels like truths
are still being argued
by citizens unknown

and undecided
straining to see justice
in the jury room's dusty light

III. Margins of Safety

Cartographical

First the water, mother of all stories. The global ocean
we can't cross on foot. Later the problem of Thuringia
and the mapping of the East. The many facts that bear repeating—
our need for cloudless nights to read stars, knowledge
of where to find water, how to heal wounds with plants.
We fan out, heads filling with mythical maps that can't see
where we are. Walking in different directions for eons,
you and I meet again, and I put you in charge
of décor. You cover our walls with maps of the world,
the heavens, ancient cities, the high Sierras.
We can go anywhere from our couch. But we part
once more, without having dared to explore
the dark. We've taken each other for maps. We've failed
to hydrate enough. We can't keep going, together.

A Seraph Speaks

—After the mosaic seraphim ("burning ones" in Hebrew) in Hagia Sophia

I can't help overhear them talking in their minds.
Like this one, complaining so much about feeling
observed, the annoying, invisible eye, inner megaphone
voice that merely repeats what she says—
I want to give it to her: Full angel. I radiate light
of the highest order, then have to wait
while she takes a bathroom break, checks
herself out in the mirror, reapplies sunblock.
Now she's back in this house of holy wisdom,
reading about me on her phone as I show
her my glorious blue-and-gold wings—two humbly
covering my feet, two crossed over my head
for protection, two outstretched to fly—all
covered with eyes. At last she looks up
and feels me burning. My body is a flame
and she's afraid. She knows she's not gawking
at peacock feathers. I tell her, Child, I'm taking time
from watching God to watch you. Let me see
you smolder, if you can't ignite.

Sister Mary Joseph Serves Lunch in Ávila

Fierce Mother Teresa and quiet Juan,
her much younger, but equally
powerful protégé, can't stop
themselves from levitating
like thousand-layer cakes
raised by inner fires
when they talk of God.

Bearing trays
of steaming *sancocho*
I see them as I pass
on my way to the refectory
where as usual
they'll be late for the meal
but perhaps in time for *flan.*

We sisters all have visions here
but only those two hang suspended
inches off the chapel floor
float light and open as plastic
sandwich bags
able to hold God's yeasty thoughts

yet overstuffed
as *Swann's Way*
with secrets that, like Marcel,
they can't help spilling
in a big mess on the tiles,
invisible dust and crumbs
we can't sweep away
from dark interiors through which Jews
are pushing up.

Teresa and Juan's sandaled feet
rest on misty shoulders
of his *padre*, her *abuelo*,
and other past and future family
members bearing books,
pens, and cans of sauerkraut

come to share today's *midrash*
ready to lift these two *converso*
mystics through the roof.

The Invention of the One God

It was a good idea on the whole. Now we get full attention.
Like us, the many gods get distracted by one another
and are prone to fighting, romantic messing, and slacking off.
The many gods, of storm, wind, earth, and so on, administer
the world. The One God mainly administers us.
We are all this deity's children, though some question
how many kids a single parent can raise.
Like two-year-olds, we want our parent to leave us
alone in a room to play with our infinite selves
until it's time for a cookie and kisses for any bruises
we may have sustained. We depend on the One God
not to beget upon us a rival, some pagan half-god sibling
who would only make trouble. We love
that the One God has only us. We scrutinize
our faces in mirrors and daily give thanks
that the One God can't be seen.

Jesus Returns to the Holy Land

I watch him disappear, back into a pre-
Christian crowd, imagine him living
in Nazareth again, near his brothers,
traveling with this wife and children
on Passover to Jerusalem.

I think he might have bad dreams,
avoid questions. A preacher who no longer
teaches, he follows Mosaic law
about doing and not doing to others.

My Jesus stays off the grid and no one
has ever heard of him.

The Lost Jewish Soul of Jesus

On the third day, the body rose, threw open
the tomb door, stepped out and inhaled,
as if it had never before breathed air.

It was primed, felt fit as a weight lifter,
ready to relish another few weeks
as a body transformed, with still a few

people to meet, a few things to say,
before it went all the way back
to Father. The new body strode forth

in triumph, absorbing the sun
and failing to see it was trailed
by its pale *neshama*, the Jewish soul

it was born with. The leftover soul
could barely keep up; this was a switch
it hadn't expected. Once breath has left,

a body is supposed to stay put, and
already, the *neshama* should have been
well on its way somewhere else, not

to Gehenna, but at least as far
as Lower Paradise. It waited,
yet the Father sent no further instructions

and the *neshama* felt it should stick
close to the new body, until the muddle
grew clearer. Soon, the body disappeared,

as if it too were a soul. Now an extra
without a script, and no one who knew
it was still on the Earth, the exhaled

neshama stayed with the Jews.

At Cousin Fanny's Table

Henry and I had been chatting at Seders
in Fanny's elegant, Upper East Side apartment
for years, but it was not until the movie version
of *Schindler's List* appeared that he revealed
what I couldn't have guessed. This urbane,
affable man, a Maurice Chevalier from Dresden
who sang show tunes while playing piano,
had survived in Krakow, along with his parents
and sister, as a member of the list. He never spoke
about his past, yet after seeing the film unearthed
his black-striped, brown, concentration camp uniform,
which not even his wife knew he'd kept.
Now, he said, he showed it to kids during talks
in New York schools. *They need to see someone*
who lived through it, standing in front of them,
to know it was real, he told us. I imagined
his uniform, deeply creased from fifty dark years
in a drawer, and wished he'd brought it here.

Henry always looked dapper, tonight in a violet
silk tie and pale linen suit. He might have a closetful
of light-weight, long-sleeved shirts to cover
his tattoo in summer. Had his drawer also hidden
his memory of hunger? He stayed trim, didn't overeat
at the Seder feast. *He weighed only eight-five pounds*
at liberation, Fanny murmured as we carried plates
from the kitchen. In camp, he said, he ate only
a daily cup of vegetable-scrap soup, a single piece
of black, moldy bread. I wanted to know more,
but didn't push. At Fanny's, we ate chicken soup,
a homemade, fatty sea afloat with matzoh balls
tender as descended clouds, drank dry red wine from Israel.

Several Seders later, when I'd just returned from Poland,
Henry said, *I'd never go back, but want very much*

to see your photos. We looked at them after dinner,
alone at the table. On the *Schindler's List* Tour, I'd photographed
the street where camp commander Goeth threw open
his window each morning to shoot prisoners.
When we came to a photo of a pharmacy on a square,

Henry stopped me. *One day there was an* aktion, he said.
I would have been rounded up, but a Nazi who knew me
was on duty and told me to go around the corner.

Watching his face, I saw him go missing behind it.
What he said was enough. I didn't need to see him suffer
like an actor in a closeup, pull out the whole dark drawer.
Fanny called us to the living room for chocolates.

How I Became a Zionist Without Really Trying

Born on the wrong side of the Jewish blanket,
all I knew of Israel growing up was not the Exodus
but my crush, on fellow half-Jew Paul Newman
as he played a full one in the movie.

My uncles were anti-Zionist Communists,
my grandparents supporters of Birobidzhan,
the Soviet version of a Jewish homeland.
My father played violin at their parties.

I fell in love with a dual-national Jew from Detroit
and then with his nine-year-old Israeli son.
Terrorists attacked schools near the kid's,
and he told me he felt like a target.

During the Gulf War, the kid put on a mask
and, surprise, my husband was called up,
ordered by the IDF to report to Fort Dix
with his reserve unit, all old men over 40.

Later the kid learned how to drive a tank,
got sent to Lebanon. In the West Bank, he checked
IDs, told me how easy it was to slip
on a mask of power in that thankless job.

My husband and I were on treadmills, watching TV,
when Rabin got shot. My beloved froze, almost fell.
Fast forward to October 7th. For failure to denounce
Israel's response, I became a Zionist to anti-Zionist pals.

Now I felt like a target myself. Short on ideology,
I was long on lived experience. Love and history
met, as I double-checked the box for chance,
wept like a Jew by the rivers of New York.

Another False Narrative

My Cossacks just left, taking with them
everything they could carry.
As usual, my books, notebooks,
my rubber crutch. I can't even climb
the walls. But deep in my closet,
a locust swarm gathers. I ride it
back to the desert, scan for signs,
a dung-beetle track, ripple of sand,
to find an oasis of laughing doves.

Scribbling again has meaning, yet certain
as ink on paper, as bullies' lies
on social media, these scimitared
thugs will return. In a garden
of sunflowers outside Odessa, my aunt
fell in love with one of the Cossacks
on horseback passing her house.

She was only four, but her story
reminds me not to be fooled
if now and then, they are handsome.
A pogrom against words is still a pogrom.

Warfare Is the Opposite of Practicing Tonglen

Asked to inhale
your pain

and to exhale
my compassion

I instead
inhale your righteous

rage
feel fear

exhale my own
just rage in return

and too fast to notice
a fiery fence

springs up
the burning barricade

of exhaled words
that separates

my dangerous pain
and yours

and makes us equal
in unsafety

Nameless

Eyes closed, waiting for sleep in a dark room,
I feel something light on one of my eyelids.
I turn on the lamp, see an insect
on my night table flap filmy wings, stretch
long, spidery legs to climb onto a book.
I don't know the word for this creature.

As an adult, playing Scrabble
with my father and sisters, I wanted to win
but always lost. They loved strategy,
I the dictionary and how, on the board,
switching two letters could utterly change
a word and its meaning.

Once, gazing at nothing through the windshield
of my parked car, I thought of our father,
cheerful nudist of our childhood home,
wondered if his unveilings counted
as incest and saw an insect
from nowhere land with a splat on the glass.

When Jung's patient recounted her dream
of gold-scarab jewelry, a real scarab flew
in through his office window.
A thing in the mind could come out.

Tonight, I can't remember whether my window
was left open or closed, but notice that
my visitor has retreated. It might
be under the bed, crawling the rug,
making its way back to a messy closet.

Near the Exit

He is dead, but his death is not dead.
　　　　　　　—David Grossman

Driving six years later, nearly at the Thornton
exit where my youngest sister met her end,

I still drop down a plumb line
to pain—only this time spot in the sky

a lone green balloon, floating way in front
and to my left. It hangs over the place

she skidded to, burning a diagonal
trail that started where I am now

and finished where she stalled. I pray
as always, that stuck sideways

in traffic, she didn't see the other
car, that couldn't stop, shifted

"heart and other organs a quarter
inch," snapped her neck.

Small as a human head, the balloon
swings away from the site, hovers

over my lane, zips toward me,
slips over my roof. I can't find it

in the rear-view mirror or pull off
to look back, so drive on, thinking

that my friend, a medium, would say,
It's a sign, this is how they speak to us.

A nanosecond later, an inner voice
intones, *Once dead, she can never*

die again, and I have to laugh
at my release. My hands relax

on the wheel, light for a moment
as one breath free of grief.

The Three of Us

What I miss most about being with my sisters
is not our talk—no one could joke or fight like us,
switch from friend to enemy and back in an instant—
but those occasions we had to be naked together,
maybe changing clothes after swimming,
getting dressed up for a wedding. Our faces
revealed we were sisters, but our bodies even more,
with breasts jutting rather than round,
nipples modestly inverted, unless it was cold
or there was something to get excited about.
Our dark, springy bushes seemed large
long before the fashion of shaving them.
They were fertile deltas-in-waiting,
the size and shape of our mother's. We three
were cut from the same warm cloth, yet none
of us bore a child, two by choice, one by bad luck.
Over time, we no longer undressed together
or traded sweaters. When we were young
I felt we could stroll between and into
one another's bodies, like houseguests
who don't need an invitation.

Getting Wings

A week before she died, my mother-in law dreamed
of her long-gone mother, come back to lead her
in the morning prayer. She'd forgotten the Hebrew
but remembered as they recited together.

I was moved to hear that the Modeh Ani,
a prayer of thanks upon waking, begins with
God, the soul you have given me is pure.
For a moment, I felt the spray of its glad fountain.

How pure can any soul be? Today I'm on a plane
heading west to help my wounded sister
and mine still feels stained, by a sin
with no seeming link to God, only to me.

The Modeh Ani goes on to say that God
restores my soul to me each morning,
a nice idea but one that implies it's borrowed
for the night. When I lay me down
to sleep and pray the Lord my soul to keep,
how safe am I without it?

Right now, I'm in my favorite space, the troposphere,
perfectly suspended over time zones.

What does God do with my soul all night?
There's always been a touch it has feared
and another it has desperately craved.

Merging

Now you have lost the sight of one eye
as well as the hearing stolen

long ago from one ear
on the opposite side

Your losses are symmetrical

and I can't stop imagining your head
full of holes

Sometimes I feel that I am you

the way I did that day we met
by surprise in a clothing store

and in that first moment thought
you were me and I you

Now I am a waterfall that can't stop
falling and I feel you falling too

I remember how as children
we sometimes dreamed the same dreams

wondered in the morning if they began
with me or you

You hadn't wanted to see me
in years

but emailed to let me know
because, you said, *You're my sister*

I cover one eye with one hand
use the other to stop hearing in one ear

Some Say the Moon Landing Was a Hoax

I understand why they don't believe in what they can't see
for themselves. I wasn't sure, until I arrived on a jet and glimpsed
the moon above Big Ben, that England was really there.

Before the astronauts landed the moon had been unreachable,
unknowable, for all of human time. As a little girl, I once reached
through an open window to grab it.

You can't touch the moon, my parents exclaimed. *It's not ours.*
And it's too far away. Now they're gone, and that shimmering
body persists. As do the boot prints the astronauts left.

Proof of Life

As a child I asked old people
for stories of their childhood.

My piano teacher
gentle Mr. Greenwood
thrillingly born on my birthday
seventy-five years before me
picked apples in Germany.

My grandma Sima waited to grow
tall as her midwife mother
while silver fir trees grew taller
around their porch in Crimea.

I trusted them for proof
that I could live.

Today I'd like to ask them if I did
or need to catch up
with the albatross winging ahead
dropping feathers.

Jesus and I Go to the Beach

We walk to the Sea of Galilee, sit in low beach chairs
on the shore, cool our bare feet in the water. The day is hot.
Climate change is upon us.

This Jesus never died and went to heaven, but I can't help
thinking of the old story. I have to ask myself:

—What exactly happened in that tomb?

—Did the contents of his body melt inside him, as in a chrysalis,
   to form the tissues of a new body?

They say he'd emerged looking just as he had before
he was broken. If a change had occurred, it remained hidden.

—And what of that ascent? Did he rise like an elevator
   or a rocket?

—How did it feel watching the earth and familiar faces grow
   smaller, ever to be seen again? Did he even look?

—And was he sorry or relieved to enter the cloud that took him
   the rest of the way? Did he mind losing his body
   for the second time? Or, did he butterfly his way back
   into heaven?

Jesus picks up a pebble, makes it skip on the lake's calm surface.
Looks at me and I see he is now much younger, and a girl.

You look like your little sister, if you had one, I say.
Jesus always could read minds. She says, Yes,
the future is female.

So how about a shawarma? And a soak at Herod's baths?
We agree.

The springs are still scalding after two thousand years and there's no time like the present. Jesus and I put our sandals back on.

Happily, hers are the right size.

What Dares Not Name Its Name

when you suspect

that what you want most
but must keep secret

especially from yourself
the sweetness

of a divine but unholy
union

that could fission you
like an atom

you learn to hide

move like a spy
through a shuttered country

you climb a ladder

nailed to the wall
of a deep dry well

seek refuge

in a dissolving
unlockable penthouse

Oh Bartleby you cry

as your tiny sun barely makes it
over the horizon

where you don't really live
although you have battled with giants

and still keep watch
for the one with a staff

encircled by a single serpent

Eve's Mother

Exiled before time began,
the Mother can be coaxed back

to Her creation with prayers
and burning candles on the Sabbath.

Rabbis have said she likes to appear
in empty spaces

upon the earth or within our souls
to fill them with Her presence

that She is attracted
to our world by *lovingkindness*

and that *bloodshed, incest, and perversions
of justice* make her depart.

Women have reported feeling
Her presence most often

in their kitchens
where, like Julia Child

late in her TV career
She likes to stand

beside a younger chef
to comment and advise.

The Virgin Mary fed her son
with her body, but was not known

for her cooking.
Eve's Mother plays

with the fruits of the earth,
can still make a mean apple pie.

Watching a grand-daughter cook
She sticks a finger into a bowl

for a taste and pronounces it good.

Note: Some of the ideas and words in this poem are taken from an essay by Rabbi Tirzah Firestone, "Relating to God Through Emptiness," published in *Gashmius*, Vol. 3.

I Draw Myself

The first drawing was a line traced around the shadow of a woman.

Old women like me should be represented with swift and furious
gestures.

A painter with clumsy hands will paint similar hands in her work.

I leave hand-prints on the wall.

About the Author

Catherine Gonick has published poetry in journals including *The Notre Dame Review, Beltway Poetry Quarterly, Pedestal, The Orchards Poetry Journal, One Art, Of The Book, The Nu Review,* and *The New Verse News.* Her work has also appeared in anthologies including *in plein air,* Poetic License Press; *Grabbed: Poets & Writers on Sexual Assault, Empowerment and Healing,* Beacon Press; *Dead of Winter 2021,* Milk & Cake Press; *Support Ukraine,* Moonstone Press; and *Rumors, Secrets & Lies: Poems About Pregnancy, Abortion and Choice,* Anhinga Press. She is a winner of the Ina Coolbrith Prize for Poetry and was a finalist in the Louisville Actors Theatre 10-Minute Play Contest. A native of California's Bay Area, she lives in the Hudson Valley with her husband, with whom she works in a company that seeks to slow the rate of global warming.

Sheila-Na-Gig Editions

www.ingramcontent.com/pod-product-compliance
Lightning Source LLC
Chambersburg PA
CBHW071207120626
46546CB00006B/2462